GROWTH MINDSET
ACTIVITIES FOR KIDS

GROWTH MINDSET ACTIVITIES FOR KIDS

55 Exercises to Embrace Learning and Overcome Challenges

Esther Pia Cordova

Illustrations by Ellen Korbonski

ROCKRIDGE
PRESS

For general information on our other products and services or to obtain technical support, please contact our Customer Care Department within the United States at (866) 744-2665, or outside the United States at (510) 253-0500.

Rockridge Press publishes its books in a variety of electronic and print formats. Some content that appears in print may not be available in electronic books, and vice versa.

Interior and Cover Designer: Michael Cook
Art Producer: Michael Hardgrove
Editor: John Makowski
Production Editor: Nora Milman

Illustration © 2020 Ellen Korbonski, Shutterstock/SylvieDesign, p. 38.

ISBN: Print 978-1-64611-768-0

Printed in Canada

R0

To Brad, who has cheerleaders in his head

Contents

A Letter to Grown-Ups

I'm grateful you are investing in your children's future and giving them the gift of a growth mindset. Empowering kids with a growth mindset when they are still young gives them an invaluable strategy for life. We can accomplish so much if we don't let our brains limit us. This book will support your child in developing and maintaining a growth mindset, and help them get rid of fixed mindset thoughts that may hold them back.

Imagine your child's thoughts going from "I can't do that" to "I can't do that, yet." A small change, but one with a great impact. In a 2007 study, children with a growth mindset were found to outperform students with a fixed mindset, especially in the face of challenges and setbacks. This simple concept helps children overcome their fears and learn as much as they can in life.

With the help of the activities and stories in this book, your kids will learn and practice embracing a growth mindset. Doing so will help supercharge their capacity to learn and grow, something we all want for our kids.

You will be impressed by the impact a new mindset will have on your child and your family. Children with a growth mindset know that success is based on hard work and learning. Intelligence and talent are not innate abilities, but rather those that can be trained and practiced. With a growth mindset, children focus on learning rather than just "looking smart," see effort as the key to success, and thrive in the face of challenges.

Along with teaching and showing kids what a growth mindset is and how we can embrace it, it is critical that we lead with our own growth mindset. As your child works on their growth mindset, you can teach by example and incorporate the following practices to help encourage a growth mindset at home:

- be mindful of your self-talk and be a role model as a learner
- continue to emphasize to your kids that their brains can get stronger and stronger
- show your kids that mistakes are an opportunity to learn and grow
- focus on the effort over the results
- teach kids that if they can't do something now, it just means that they can't do it, *yet*
- be specific with your praise

Kids learn the most from imitating the people they love the most—that's you! It's also helpful for your child to know about your own struggles with having a growth mindset. We can't always be positive and never have any fixed mindset thoughts—that's okay and part of the idea of embracing a growth mindset. Encouraging a growth mindset in your child is a lifelong process. By helping them approach things from a different perspective, this book will give your child some great tools with which to achieve their dreams.

A Letter to Kids

Welcome, kids!

We are going to have a lot of fun with this book. Each chapter starts with a short story before diving into exciting activities that will help you learn about and develop a growth mindset.

Kids with a fixed mindset believe that they're born with a certain set of talents and intelligence, but kids with a growth mindset know that they can always train and improve their skills and abilities. With hard practice, you can actually grow your brain!

Kids with a growth mindset know that they can learn and achieve a lot by:

- Working hard
- Practicing creativity
- Trying different things
- Not being afraid of making mistakes
- Asking for help when they need it

Through fun activities, we'll practice each of these skills step by step. The focus will be on the fun, but you'll also be learning important skills to help you become whatever you want to be. Remember, it is not about *being* the best; it is about *doing* your best!

I'm excited to go on this journey with you. Let the fun begin!

CHAPTER ONE

I CAN DO IT!

The Big Game

Juan loves all sports, but basketball is his favorite. He practices with his dad every afternoon. Today at school, Juan's class got to play softball. Juan was the first player at bat. His friend Josie was the pitcher, and she threw the first ball. The ball came straight toward Juan. He got in position, swung, and missed. *Oh no, I missed*, thought Juan. Josie didn't wait long and quickly threw a second ball right toward Juan. *WHOOSH*.

I missed again. Maybe I'm just not good at this. Juan had so many thoughts at once, and he felt his face get hot. Before his third try, Juan took a deep breath, looked into the sky, and thought about the times he played sports with his dad.

Juan remembered how proud his father gets when they practice basketball, so he was determined to try to do his best at bat. Ready for the third ball, Juan gave Josie a nod, and she threw the ball. The ball was quick, and Juan swung as hard as he could. But he missed the third ball. Now he was convinced that he simply was no good at softball.

The rest of the game was a blur. After the game, he went to the class fridge and got his favorite snack: some celery sticks with a jar of peanut butter. As he ate, he remembered the first time he practiced playing basketball with his dad. He remembered that he couldn't reach the basket, and that his dad lowered the hoop for Juan. He remembered not being very good, but he always had so much fun playing anyway. Juan smiled and said to himself, "I will get better at softball. I just need to practice, focus, and keep trying. I will learn to hit the ball. Watch out, Josie!"

What Is a Growth Mindset?

The way we think is flexible. We can think of so many different things. We call the way we think a "mindset." There are two different kinds of mindsets: **fixed mindset** and **growth mindset**. Kids with a fixed mindset believe that intelligence and talent are abilities they are born with, and kids with a growth mindset know that success comes from hard work and learning. At the beginning of the story, Juan had a lot of fixed mindset thoughts like "I'm not good at softball." After thinking more about it, Juan's thinking switched into more of a growth mindset way of thinking, because he remembered getting better at basketball by practicing.

Here's an example of growth mindset thinking versus fixed mindset thinking:

FIXED MINDSET	GROWTH MINDSET
Believes that intelligence and talent are abilities kids are born with.	Knows that intelligence and talent are abilities that can change with time and effort.
"I'm just not good at this."	"I will learn to do this."
"I'm bad at math."	"I'm going to get better at math."
"I'm not good at softball."	"I will get better if I concentrate, practice, and keep trying."

What's My Mindset?

Now you know that a growth mindset is all about improving and getting better over time. Kids with a growth mindset focus on learning instead of just looking smart. They know they have to keep trying to get better, and they don't give up when there's a challenge.

WHAT YOU NEED

- markers or colored pencils

DIRECTIONS

1. Look at the following statements and color the face that shows best how you feel about this statement today: agree (happy), not sure (neutral), or disagree (sad). Be as honest as you can! Each face will give you points.
2. Add all the points together to get your final number.

STATEMENTS	AGREE - NOT SURE - DISAGREE
"When something is hard, I want to work on it more."	☺ 😐 ☹
"I can always improve, so I keep trying."	☺ 😐 ☹
"I can train my brain."	☺ 😐 ☹
"I have no problem making mistakes."	☺ 😐 ☹

"It's okay when things don't work for me right away."	🙂	😐	🙁
"I love seeing others succeed."	🙂	😐	🙁
"I can get smarter when I work hard."	🙂	😐	🙁
"Mistakes help me learn better."	🙂	😐	🙁
"I can learn anything I want to."	🙂	😐	🙁
"I like to learn new things even when I make mistakes."	🙂	😐	🙁

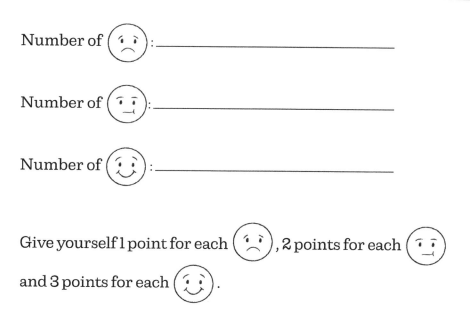

Number of 🙁 : _____

Number of 😐 : _____

Number of 🙂 : _____

Give yourself 1 point for each 🙁 , 2 points for each 😐 and 3 points for each 🙂 .

Growth Mindset points: _____

GROWTH MINDSET EXPERT (24–30 POINTS)	You already have a growth mindset! You know that the right mindset helps you achieve your goals and dreams. When it gets hard, you stay positive and focus on your growth mindset. Great job! You also know how important practice is for a growth mindset. This book will help you stick with your can-do mindset and grow some of your ideas even more.
GROWTH MINDSET WARRIOR (17–23 POINTS)	This is a great starting point! You already have some great growth mindset ideas in your head. That's great! This book will help you grow these ideas and make your growth mindset even stronger.
GROWTH MINDSET STARTER (10–16 POINTS)	You are a Growth Mindset Starter! The great thing is you can have the biggest and quickest growth of all the categories. I'm excited for you to go on this growth mindset journey. Remember, you can always improve! Keep reading, keep practicing, and you will soon amaze yourself!

MY GROWTH MINDSET TAKEAWAY

There are no right or wrong answers. This is just one way of measuring your starting point. At the end of this book, we will look at these statements again and you will see how your mindset changed through practice and effort.

Water My Thoughts

Having a fixed mindset like Juan did in the beginning of the story is not helpful for getting better or feeling good!

Having positive thoughts and knowing that you can get better at things with time and effort can help you feel stronger. This is true for all areas of your life. Think of your thoughts like a budding plant. We can "water" or grow our growth mindset thoughts and not let the weeds of fixed mindset ideas take over our thinking!

WHAT YOU NEED

- a pencil

DIRECTIONS

Look at the following thoughts. Water the growth mindset thoughts by drawing water drops around them, and then cross out the fixed mindset thoughts.

"I'm bad.
I give up."

"I made a mistake, but
next time I will do it
better."

"It's going to take
some time and effort."

"I can't do it, yet."

"I will never be
able to read well."

"This is too hard."

"I'm getting a little
better every day."

"It's impossible."

REMEMBER

Switching your mindset can be hard. But with time and practice, you can do it!

MY GROWTH MINDSET TAKEAWAY

It's normal to have some fixed mindset thoughts like "I'm not good at math." But we can give growth mindset thoughts room to grow. We can easily go from "I'm not good at math" to "I'm not good at math, *yet*!"

Positive or Negative Self-Talk?

Have you ever noticed an inner voice talking to you? That voice in your head that says you can (or can't) do something? This is your conscience giving you self-talk, and it's totally normal! Let's explore it.

WHAT YOU NEED

- a pencil

DIRECTIONS

Let's look at some self-talk messages and decide if they show a growth or fixed mindset. Read through the following statements and check the box you think is true.

SELF-TALK SENTENCES	GROWTH MINDSET	FIXED MINDSET
1. "I can't do this because I'm dumb."		
2. "I did a great job."		
3. "This is difficult, but I can kind of do it."		
4. "I can't do this, yet."		
5. "I am proud of myself."		
6. "They don't want to be my friend because I'm stupid."		
7. "I'm the worst ever."		
8. "I hate this."		

9. "My friend is so good at math, but with practice I will be, too."		
10. "I'm no good at this."		
11. "I will never get that right!"		
12. "I will keep trying."		
13. "I love this challenge!"		
14. "One day, I will be able to do it."		
15. "Everyone will think I'm crazy."		
16. "It's not good yet, but I will spend more time improving."		
17. "I am so ugly."		
18. "My head hurts from thinking hard, but I can see the progress I made."		
19. "I am so stupid."		
20. "This is hard, but with practice I can do it."		

MY GROWTH MINDSET TAKEAWAY

Sometimes your inner voice will talk to you in a supportive, positive way, and sometimes in a discouraging, negative way. It's important to notice your inner voice. Once you are aware of it, you can shift your thinking from negative messages to more positive ones.

Inner Voice Interview

Everybody has an inner voice—even grown-ups! Some people have very loud voices that talk to them all the time. That can be overwhelming and exhausting. Other people have calmer inner voices. Sometimes we have positive little cheerleader voices, and other times, it's negative "Debbie Downer" voices.

WHAT YOU NEED

* a pencil
* a grown-up

DIRECTIONS

Interview an adult, such as a family member or family friend. Ask them about their "inner voice."

REMEMBER

Talking about our inner thoughts and voices is very personal. Some people never share anything about what is going on in their heads. It's brave to share and be open and honest. This honesty helps us improve. It also helps us be aware of our inner thoughts when we share them with others.

MY GROWTH MINDSET TAKEAWAY

The voices in our heads are created by us! They seem separate from us, but we can learn to control what and how much these voices are telling us. This is a fascinating topic!

We can't see or hear one another's inner voices, but we know everybody has them. Your neighbor, your parents, your teacher, and even the store cashier all have inner voices. You may have heard that you should talk to yourself "like you would to a friend." This is great advice, but sometimes it can be hard. It can take lots of practice to make your thoughts positive. Some days this will be easier, and some days it will be harder. But the more you practice, the better you'll get!

Interview: Inner Voices

Name: _____

Are your inner voices usually loud and all over the place, or calm?

Calm 1   2   3   4   5   6   7   8   9   10   **Loud**

What is something your inner voice said you couldn't do but you did anyway? How did this make you feel?

_____

_____

Did your inner voice change after you did this?

_____

When is your inner voice the happiest?

_____

When is your inner voice the saddest?

_____

What do you do to calm your inner voice when it gets too loud or
negative?

_____

Sharing Inner Voices

Let's work with an adult partner to share our inner voices.

WHAT YOU NEED

- 2 pens or pencils
- an adult partner

DIRECTIONS

Ask an adult to take 30 minutes in which both of you will pay attention to what your inner voice is telling you. On the next page, write down all the thoughts without judging them. Try to find at least three thoughts you want to talk about. Then do the following activities together:

1. Decide if each thought is a growth or fixed mindset.
2. Talk about how you felt when you had that thought.
3. For each fixed mindset thought, come up with a growth mindset thought you could change it to.

For example, you might think, "I'm not good at reading," but with the tiny but powerful word "yet," you can turn this sentence into a growth mindset sentence ("I'm not good at reading, *yet*").

REMEMBER

Be open and brave. Writing your personal thoughts down and sharing them can be a little awkward or scary at first, but you can do it!

MY GROWTH MINDSET TAKEAWAY

It's reassuring to know that everybody has an inner voice. And everybody has fixed mindset thoughts from time to time—that's okay. All we need to do is be aware of these thoughts and remember to reword them as something more positive!

_____

_____

_____

_____

_____

_____

_____

Spot the Mindset

Growth mindset thoughts can be found in everyday life. Can you identify which mindset the kids have in the following pictures?

WHAT YOU NEED

- a pencil

DIRECTIONS

1. Look at the following pictures. Decide which kid has a growth mindset and which has a fixed mindset.
2. Write down their mindsets as headlines over each picture.

MY GROWTH MINDSET TAKEAWAY

Life is busy. It can be hard to always be aware of which mindset is taking over. When things get hard, take a deep breath and see if you can figure out which mindset your inner voice is following.

Sort My Thoughts

Let's sort our inner thoughts into categories!

WHAT YOU NEED

- two containers (jars, resealable containers, or boxes)—one container will hold growth mindset thoughts and the other will hold fixed mindset thoughts
- 15 small items of your choice (buttons, balls, pennies, building blocks, etc.)

DIRECTIONS

1. Label the two containers "Growth Mindset" and "Fixed Mindset."
2. Choose statements from the list on page 18 that mean something to you. It can be something that happens a lot. You can also get creative and make up your own statements. For example, "I go to basketball practice once a week."
3. Read the statements out loud and then say out loud the very first thought that comes to your mind. There is no right or wrong answer—just say whatever pops into your head! For example, "I love hockey practice. I'm getting better at skating."
4. Decide if that thought was a growth or fixed mindset thought, and then place one token in the matching container.

LIST OF STATEMENTS

- "We will have a math test tomorrow."
- "Let's do an unannounced spelling test."
- "You will need to show the class a handstand."
- "You forgot your homework for the second time this week."
- "Your piano lesson starts in five minutes."
- "You need to read the first chapter out loud."
- "Let's go on a bicycle ride."
- "Let's clean up."
- "Let's have pizza!"
- "You forgot your gym clothes."
- "Please show everybody your dance moves."
- "You will get your flu shot tomorrow."
- "You lost the game."
- "You fell off your bicycle."
- "You spilled the milk."

MY GROWTH MINDSET TAKEAWAY

Are you getting better at noticing your inner thoughts and thinking about them? If so, you're on your way! Just noticing them is the first step to changing them toward a more positive direction.

CHAPTER TWO

MY BRAIN IS AMAZING!

Bigger Books

It's homework time! Evie's teacher wants her to write about her favorite book, *A World Without Failures*. That's easy for Evie. She writes how the main character, David, imagines a world where no mistakes are possible. But then in the story, all the cool stuff disappears. No TVs, no refrigerator, and not even the house—everything is gone! Why? Because nothing would have been invented if mistakes were not allowed.

After finishing her homework, Evie asks her mom about her favorite book. Her mom gives Evie one of her big mystery novels. Evie opens it, and the first thing she notices is that there are no pictures. Not even one! It's the biggest book on the shelf and the biggest book she's ever tried to read. Because it's her mom's favorite book, though, Evie wants to try to read it.

The long words make Evie's head hurt, and she can't even sound some of them out. Evie gets frustrated, but her mom reminds her of David, the little boy in Evie's favorite book. Evie and her mom say out loud, "I can't do it yet, but I can train my brain!" Proud and excited, Evie and her mom read the first two pages together. Her mom tells her what the bigger words mean. They decide that they will try to read the book every day until it's finished.

I Can Train My Brain

Your brain is like a muscle. Fact: If you try challenging your brain with hard problems, you are exercising it so it can get stronger. That makes *you* smarter and stronger. Remember, it's okay to make mistakes. The important thing is that you don't give up. If you keep trying again and again, your brain will grow!

Brain Tour

Our brain is the most complex and important organ that we have. It's responsible for all our thoughts and actions. Without our brains, we wouldn't be the people we are. Imagine your brain like a video game, and your body like the console. Without the game (your brain) inside, the console (your body) can't run!

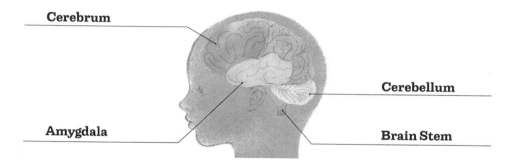

Cerebrum

Cerebellum

Amygdala

Brain Stem

Let's get to know our amazing brain a little better by looking at four of its main parts.

Cerebrum (say: *suh-REE-brum*) The cerebrum is the biggest part of our brain. The cerebrum helps us THINK and solve problems. Our memory is also stored here. The cerebrum is divided in two halves, the right and the left side. The funny thing is that the right side of your cerebrum controls the left side of your body, and the left side of your cerebrum controls the right side of your body!

Cerebellum (say: *sair-uh-BELL-um*) The cerebellum is much smaller than the cerebrum and helps you MOVE. Because of the cerebellum, you can keep yourself balanced on a bicycle and stand upright.

Amygdala (say: *ah-MIG-duh-luh*) The amygdala is a little almond-shaped structure that controls your emotions and feelings. Without the amygdala, you wouldn't be able to FEEL the difference between failing a test and winning a soccer game!

Brain Stem Your brain stem does work without you noticing. This part makes you BREATHE and keeps your heart pumping without you having to think about it. Pretty cool, don't you think?

WHAT YOU NEED

- a pencil

DIRECTIONS

Connect the parts of the brain that control the actions in the pictures.

MY GROWTH MINDSET TAKEAWAY

Now you know what the cerebrum, cerebellum, amygdala, and brain stem are doing in your brain. You're smarter already!

What Does 86 Billion Look Like?

All over our brains, we have these tiny little cells called neurons. These neurons transport information between each other. Our whole brain is connected through these little brain cells. They may be small, but there are 86 billion of them! It's hard to picture what 86 billion looks like, but let's try!

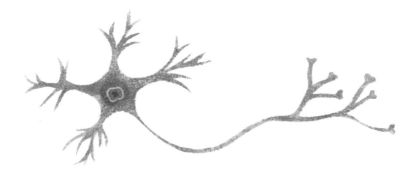

WHAT YOU NEED

- a pencil
- a grown-up to help
- Internet access

DIRECTIONS

Compare your **86 billion neurons** to these other things that there are a lot of:

- **29,000** *grains of rice in a pound*
- **18 million** *hot dogs sold at major league baseball stadiums each year*
- **600 million** *cats in the world*

- **900 million** dogs in the world
- **2.5 billion** video gamers around the world
- **7.6 billion** people in the world
- **15 billion** inches from Earth to the moon (average distance)

What number comparisons can you come up with? Work with a grown-up to search some possibilities on the Internet:

_____

_____

_____

_____

MY GROWTH MINDSET TAKEAWAY

With 86 billion neurons, think of how powerful our brains are! According to an article on NationalGeographic.com, the human brain is "the most complex structure in the universe"—that means it's more complex than the biggest, greatest, or fastest machines ever built. With that kind of power, doesn't it make sense that we can do ANYTHING we put our 86 billion neurons to work to do?

What's Good for My Brain?

Our brain is the most important organ in our body. Just like how going to the gym can help your body stay healthy, you can help your brain stay healthy by doing the following things:

- **Eat healthy foods like fresh vegetables and fruits.** These foods contain a lot of vitamins and minerals that are good for your brain. Some foods are actually called brain food! These include berries, avocados, eggs, nuts, seeds, broccoli, and oily fish like salmon.
- **Train your brain by practicing hard tasks.** Practicing things that make you think help make your brain stronger—it's like giving your brain a workout!
- **Drink plenty of water.** Three-quarters of your brain is made of water, so keeping your body hydrated with water is important.
- **Stay active!** Your brain loves when you move around and spend time outside.
- **Remember to wear a helmet.** When riding a bike or playing sports, wearing a helmet will protect your brain!

There are also things that are not so good for your brain like:

- **too much screen time**
- **drugs and alcohol**
- **sugary drinks like soda**
- **not enough sleep**

WHAT YOU NEED

- a pencil

DIRECTIONS

Try to get from one side of the maze to the other by avoiding the things that are not so good for your brain, *and* without taking your pencil off the page! If you do, then you have to start over!

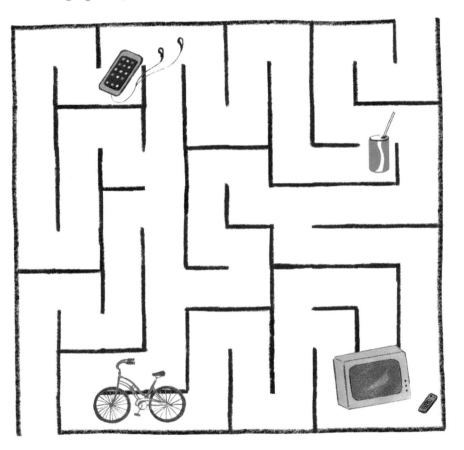

MY GROWTH MINDSET TAKEAWAY

Now you know some things you can do to keep your brain healthy. Take care of your brain so your brain can take care of you!

We're All Connected!

We learned earlier in this chapter that our brains are full of neurons. But did you know that whenever we learn something new, new connections are built between neurons? With 86 billion neurons in the brain, that means there are a LOT of possible connections!

WHAT YOU NEED

- paper and a pen
- some friends and a ball of yarn (optional)

DIRECTIONS

1. Draw 10 dots on a piece of paper. Each dot represents a neuron. When you draw a line between two dots, that's one connection made between them, just like the neurons in your brain.
2. Now try and make as many connections as possible.

You can also complete this activity with a group of friends and a ball of yarn.

DIRECTIONS FOR FOUR OR MORE KIDS:

1. Each child will represent a neuron and the yarn will show the connections. The children will stand in a circle, arm's length apart.
2. Have one child start by holding on to the end of the yarn and hand over the rest of the yarn to another person. Then they'll give it to someone else, still holding on to their part

of the yarn. Keep doing this until the yarn is completely unraveled or you run out of moves. No connection is allowed to be done twice!

Example: If Marc already gave the yarn to Sophie, Marc can't give it back to Sophie again. Also, Sophie can't give the yarn back to Marc.

Now imagine how much yarn and how many connections there would be with 86 billion neurons!

MY GROWTH MINDSET TAKEAWAY

Have you started to wrap your head around how many possible connections can be made in your brain? Our brains are like powerful computers, and they are just waiting for us to feed them information! The more connections you form by practicing and repetition, the stronger your brain will become.

My Brain Can Make Dreams a Reality

Our brain is a muscle. We know that the more we practice and challenge our brain, the stronger it gets. By practicing anything, we can develop our skills and get better and better over time. Those neurons in our brains will form a lot of connections so we can improve. With practice and hard work, you can be an expert in anything you choose—so what do *you* choose?

WHAT YOU NEED

- paper
- colored pencils

DIRECTIONS

1. Think about what you want to be an expert of. Why do you want to be an expert in this area?
2. Imagine yourself in the future when you are this expert. What will you look like? Draw a picture of your future self on a piece of paper.
3. What could you practice now that will help you become this expert?

MY GROWTH MINDSET TAKEAWAY

Skills are not abilities we are born with, or abilities that we can't change. With practice and hard work, we can train our brains to get better and better—at anything we want!

Color My Brain

Your brain has been busy at work, and this activity will see what you remember about your brain!

WHAT YOU NEED

- crayons or colored pencils

DIRECTIONS

See if you can remember which part of the brain is which by labeling and coloring the picture below. Don't worry if you don't remember the correct parts on your first try. You can go back to page 23 and look up the right parts.

1. Cerebrum - yellow
2. Cerebellum - blue
3. Brain stem - green
4. Amygdala - red

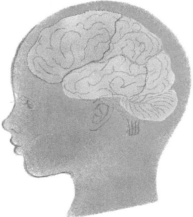

MY GROWTH MINDSET TAKEAWAY

Repetition (practice) is a great way to learn things. Now you've reminded yourself where the individual parts of the brain are located. Good for you!

CHAPTER THREE

I CAN MAKE MISTAKES!

Math Madness

"I'm just not a math person!" Ben shouted. That's the first thing his mom and dad heard from Ben after he came home from school and opened the front door. No hugs, no kisses, not even a hello.

"Hello, Ben," his mom said. "It's nice to see you, too. Do you want to tell us what happened in school?"

"No," Ben whispered.

"Well . . ." his mom started. "Let me guess. You got yesterday's quiz back and you are unhappy with the result."

Ben looked at his feet and stumbled. "Not happy . . . Well . . . I failed. I'm just not a math person. I can't do it."

His dad responded, "I can see that you're frustrated because you're learning something new, and that's hard. But did you really do your best?"

"I'm not sure," Ben replied. "I quickly finished the questions because I saw how hard they were. I just don't think I'm talented at math."

Ben's mom got up off the sofa and said, "Maybe you can't do some of the math problems yet, but if you work at it, with time and effort, you'll be able to do it! What do you think? How could you get better at math?"

Ben looked at both of his parents and said, "Maybe we could practice together after my piano lessons so I can do better for the test next week?"

"Yes!" exclaimed his dad, smiling. He hugged Ben, and they popped the good news on him—pizza for dinner!

I Can Learn from My Mistakes

Even though mistakes can make you feel upset when they happen, they also help you learn and grow. Mistakes show us how we can improve and keep learning. When you make a mistake, ask yourself these three questions:

1. What went wrong?
2. What could I do better next time?
3. What did I learn from this?

Sometimes your mistakes can tell you that you need to put in more effort, try harder, or slow down. Looking at your mistakes and learning from them is a great way to do better!

Activity 14

Can I Control It?

Can you relate to Ben? We sometimes feel upset or annoyed when things don't turn out the way we want. Sometimes these feelings turn into frustration. Frustration can happen when we feel like we can't change or achieve something. But sometimes we get frustrated about things that we *can* change. That's the time to step up! When you feel frustrated, stop and check if the things that frustrate you are things you can control or not control.

WHAT YOU NEED
- paper
- scissors
- colored pencils
- glue stick
- a friend or family member

DIRECTIONS
1. Take two pieces of paper and draw a huge bucket on each of them. Label one of the buckets "I CAN control" and the other "I CAN'T control."
2. Now cut out four (or more) small cards and write on the empty cards two things that you think are outside of your control and two things that are inside your control. Glue the cards to the correct bucket. Some ideas can include:

- The weather
- What other people say
- Your talents
- Your behavior
- Your skin color
- What others think
- Being kind
- Your skills
- Loving yourself
- Working hard
- How you treat others
- Being sick

3. Think about the cards in the "I CAN'T control" bucket. Is there any way you can move them to the "I CAN control" bucket? Chat with a friend or family member about the possibilities.

REMEMBER

Put yourself in the situation described on each of these cards. Then think: Is there anything you could do to improve the situation now or in the future? If you're not sure, ask a friend. Of course, some things are always out of our control. We can't change the weather just because we want to!

MY GROWTH MINDSET TAKEAWAY

This next time you are frustrated, take a deep breath. Think about your frustration. Is it maybe outside of your control? If it's really outside of your control, then try the next activity—it can help!

Make Lemonade

Have you ever heard the saying "When life hands you lemons, make lemonade"? It means that if something is outside of your control, you can still change the way you look at it!

WHAT YOU NEED

- a pencil or colored pencils

DIRECTIONS

1. Look at the following pictures. How can the situation be made better? Draw something to help the characters deal with the situation.
2. Next, think of two situations that maybe you can't change, but you could change the way you think about them.

MY GROWTH MINDSET TAKEAWAY

Some things in life can make us feel frustrated when we can't change them, but we can ALWAYS change our mindset and how we look at things!

Activity 16

A World Without Mistakes

Making mistakes can make us feel frustrated. How cool would it be to live in a world without mistakes?

WHAT YOU NEED

- a pencil

DIRECTIONS

1. Imagine a world with no mistakes. Write down and think (or talk with a partner) about the things that never would have to happen again. Think about how nobody would ever spill milk again or forget their gym clothes! What else can you think of?

_____

_____

_____

2. Go through the following list and decide if these items would be possible if nobody was allowed to make any mistakes. Remember: It takes lots of trial and error (mistakes) to come up with a working invention!

ITEM	WOULD NOT EXIST	WOULD EXIST
apples		
clothes		
phones		
supermarkets		
stones		
houses		
electricity		
the sun		
glasses		
refrigerators		
Internet		

1. What item would you miss the most? Would that item be possible in a world without mistakes?

_____

2. Do you want to live in a world without mistakes?   Yes / No

MY GROWTH MINDSET TAKEAWAY

We can practice looking at mistakes as a great way to learn. Making mistakes is how we improve and get better. Without mistakes, the world would have no learning, no inventions, no way to grow!

Let's Share Our Mistakes!

Let's brainstorm together about the mistakes we made last week. Then let's embrace those mistakes—that means to accept and even love them! And we all make mistakes, so don't be afraid to share them. Through mistakes, we learn.

WHAT YOU NEED

- a partner

DIRECTIONS

Think about last week. Choose one mistake you made and talk about it with your partner, then switch and let them tell you about a mistake they made. Think and talk together about what you can learn from your mistakes.

REMEMBER

Fact: Everyone makes mistakes! So who do you think is braver: the person who won't admit their mistake or the person who says, "Oh well, I made a mistake"?

MY GROWTH MINDSET TAKEAWAY

This activity helps you see mistakes as a learning opportunity. By sharing this activity with a friend, you are doing three awesome things. You are:

1. Being brave and admitting you made a mistake
2. Working together to find the lessons in each mistake
3. Getting comfortable talking about your mistakes with others!

Activity 18

Helpful Feedback vs. Unhelpful Feedback

Sometimes when we make mistakes, we don't know what went wrong! Feedback, or suggestions, from others can help us learn more about our mistakes and improve upon them. We call this constructive feedback. Destructive or unkind feedback, on the other hand, is not helpful and only hurts the other person.

WHAT YOU NEED

- a pencil

DIRECTIONS

Look through all the feedback below and cross out the feedback that is not helpful.

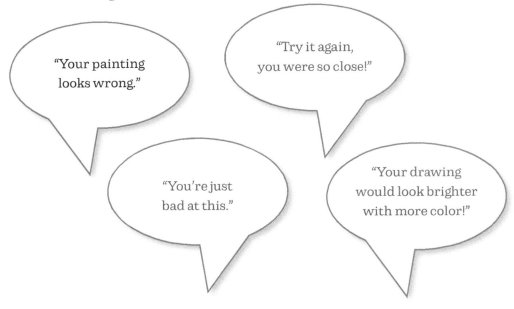

"Your painting looks wrong."

"Try it again, you were so close!"

"You're just bad at this."

"Your drawing would look brighter with more color!"

REMEMBER

We can grow and help others grow by receiving and giving helpful feedback.

Unhelpful feedback just makes people feel bad and doesn't solve anything.

Sometimes **no feedback** is the best answer—if someone draws a picture and you don't like it, you don't need to give feedback at all. They might not want to hear how you think their picture could be improved!

But if someone draws a picture and complains that they're not happy with it, then **helpful feedback** such as "Why don't you try coloring it in?" can really help!

MY GROWTH MINDSET TAKEAWAY

Try to give constructive feedback when others need or ask for help. This way, you can help the other person grow!

My Happy Mistake Growth Mindset Jar!

Mistakes are a great learning opportunity, but sometimes it's still hard to deal with mistakes and criticism. That's why today, we are building a Happy Mistake Growth Mindset Jar!

WHAT YOU NEED

- paper
- colored pencils
- a big jar or container
- decorations for the jar (stickers, pictures, positive messages, etc.)

DIRECTIONS

1. On a piece of paper, write 10 growth mindset statements. (For example: "I can't do _____, yet," "Mistakes help me grow," "I can do hard things," "I can try new things," "I'm a problem solver," "I can train my brain," "I'm getting better at reading," etc.)
2. Cut the statements and fold them in half.
3. Put them in your jar.
4. Decorate your jar.

5. Whenever you feel down, upset, or frustrated after making a mistake, take out a statement from your jar and read it out loud to yourself.

6. Refill your jar with new messages as often as you need to!

MY GROWTH MINDSET TAKEAWAY

When you get frustrated, your Happy Mistake Growth Mindset Jar will remind you that you are awesome and you are learning! We all make mistakes, but it's how we think about them that matters. Be your own positive number-one fan!

CHAPTER FOUR

MY MISTAKES CAN BE GREAT!

Dragon Dog

This is going to be awesome, thinks Mari. After watching an amazing TV show with lots of dragons, she decides to draw a fire-breathing dragon. Mari thinks that the dragon should have big beautiful wings, but she does not quite know how to draw them. She looks up several images of dragons. They are very detailed. "This is going to be hard," Mari mumbles, "but I will try." Before drawing the difficult claws and wings, Mari chooses the red crayon and starts with the most fun part, the FIRE. It looks great! But after finishing the fire, Mari notices that there's not enough space for the wings. For a few seconds, she thinks about how she could try to erase the crayon, but then she comes up with an even better idea.

Instead of the claws, Mari adds normal paws and decides that it's going to be an awesome fire-breathing dog! She takes the drawing from the table and sticks it on the fridge. Maybe it's not a dragon, but it's a pretty good dog! What a funny and happy accident!

Happy Accidents

Mari didn't start out planning to draw a cool fire-breathing dog. But instead of just giving up and being sad that her dragon didn't turn out the way she'd hoped for, she made the best of her drawing. And the drawing turned out even better than she'd planned; after all, a fire-breathing dog is much more unique and special than a dragon.

Happy accidents can happen all the time if we don't get hung up on our mistakes and failures. Happy accidents give us ways to learn from them. With effort and practice, Mari will soon be able to draw a fire-breathing dragon. On her way to getting there, she created a cool fire-breathing dog!

From Accident to Happy Accident

Happy accidents can happen all the time. Sometimes we just don't know they happen. Mari had a rough time with a few little accidents and mistakes, but instead of getting down and upset, she made the best of it, and even had fun with it.

WHAT YOU NEED

- a pencil or colored pencils

DIRECTIONS

1. Look at the following situations and imagine what could happen next to turn the accident into a happy accident.
2. Draw what happens next in the empty box and write about it.
3. Use the last boxes to draw and write about a happy accident that happened to you.

Mari is late for the school bus, and then she remembers that she forgot her gym bag at home.

_____

_____

_____

	_____
Mari accidentally calls her grandmother instead of her aunt.	_____
At night, Mari notices that she accidentally took her friend Anna's library bag instead of her own. Now she can't read the new books she wanted. None of the books inside Anna's bag seem interesting to her.	_____
	_____

MY GROWTH MINDSET TAKEAWAY

Accidents and mistakes are part of everyday life. What is important is how we look at these situations and learn how we can make the most out of them, just like Mari did. Sometimes we are lucky, and an accident can turn into a happy accident!

We Can Grow When We Fail

Sometimes we feel sad or angry when we fail. With a growth mindset, we know that failure is an important part of learning. There are amazing chances for us to grow when we fail.

The author of *Harry Potter*, J. K. Rowling, failed 12 times before she finally found a publisher who believed in her story and helped publish the book. Before that, she was told 12 different times that her story was not good enough. Good thing she did not stop trying! If she did, we would have never known Harry Potter.

WHAT YOU NEED

- paper and a pencil

DIRECTIONS

1. Imagine yourself as one of the 12 publishers who rejected the story of Harry Potter. The publishers failed, too, because they did not see the magic in the story. Why do you think they did not accept J. K. Rowling's story? Try to come up with three reasons.

2. The publishers who rejected the story of Harry Potter must have been really disappointed once they saw the success of the story. They may feel sorry that they didn't give it a chance. If you were one of these publishers, what do you think you could learn from this mistake? What would you do differently next time?

MY GROWTH MINDSET TAKEAWAY

Like *Harry Potter,* the world is full of failures that can be turned into successes. We should never let our failures or anyone's opinion hold us back. The author failed, but she did not give up until somebody accepted her book—and now it's world famous! Even the publishers who rejected *Harry Potter* might also have turned their failures into huge successes. Hopefully they know about the growth mindset!

Play It Out!

You probably know about the five senses: sight, hearing, taste, touch, and smell. But did you know that our brains learn the best if we include as many senses as possible? Today, we are going to act out our thoughts, which is a great way to use our senses—we are putting our whole selves into the role!

WHAT YOU NEED

- a little free space for acting

DIRECTIONS

Choose five of the fixed mindset statements on the left side of the following list. Come up with something you can relate to in each of these statements—maybe something that has happened to either you or someone you know—and reenact it. Then do the same thing with five of the growth mindset statements on the right side of the list. Get creative and make it fun!

Example: *"All my friends are better than me."* → *"I will try to learn from my friends."*

1. **Fixed mindset:** Act out not being able to ride a bicycle and just watch the other kids having fun and riding their bicycles.

2. **Growth mindset:** Act out not being able to ride a bicycle and then asking your friends to help you learn how to ride. Imagine that one friend has a low-riding bike that you feel safe practicing on. You borrow it and begin to learn!

FIXED MINDSET	GROWTH MINDSET
"I can't do this."	"I can take a risk and try this first."
"This is/was dumb."	"I can change how I act. Let's try again!"
"This grade means that I am brilliant."	"I practiced a lot and now it shows."
"I don't know what to do."	"What can I try to do on my own?"
"All my friends are better than me."	"I will try to learn from my friends."
"It's too hard!"	"This may take some time and effort."
"This is good enough."	"Is this the best I can do?"
"I'm really bad at this!"	"I am still learning how to do this, and that's okay."
"I make too many mistakes."	"Mistakes help me learn."
"I already know everything."	"How can I learn more?"
"This grade means that I am dumb."	"This grade means I need to put in more effort."

MY GROWTH MINDSET TAKEAWAY

Growth mindset is all about practicing and improving. By acting out the differences between a fixed and growth mindset, you can see how they work and how they make you feel. A fixed mindset means you've decided you can't do something, and so you sit on the sidelines and don't get any better. That doesn't feel so good! A growth mindset means you've decided to take a chance. You might make mistakes or fail, but if you keep trying, you can get better—which feels great!

Color My Growth

Coloring is fun, plus it can calm your mind and help you focus. This coloring page includes space to write your own growth mindset affirmation. An affirmation is a sentence that supports and encourages you.

We've learned a lot about embracing our mistakes and learning from them. This coloring page will help remind and encourage you whenever you forget. Color it your way and hang it somewhere where you can look at it every day!

WHAT YOU NEED

- colored pencils
- tape

DIRECTIONS

1. Color the coloring page with bright colored pencils. Add your own growth mindset affirmation in the center of the drawing.
2. Cut the page out of the book and hang it somewhere where you can look at it every day.

MY GROWTH MINDSET TAKEAWAY

Here's a beautiful reminder to embrace a growth mindset every day, even when it's hard.

My Failures Are My Success

"I've lost almost 300 games. Twenty-six times, I've been trusted to take the game-winning shot and missed. I've failed over and over and over again in my life. And that is why I succeed."

—**Michael Jordan**, former NBA basketball player and Hall of Famer

WHAT YOU NEED

* a partner

DIRECTIONS

1. Read the quote above and talk to your partner about how you think Michael Jordan feels about failures.
2. Now think about a few times in your life when you failed but used that failure to succeed. Take turns sharing these moments with your partner.

MY GROWTH MINDSET TAKEAWAY

This activity helps us rethink how we feel about failures. We've learned how failures are one way of learning—they can also be a way to succeed!

My "Face the Fear" Mind Map

It's normal to be afraid to fail at something. The important thing is to think about what you want to accomplish and then face your fear and do it anyway! We'll do an activity that shows you how.

WHAT YOU NEED

- a pencil or pen
- red marker

DIRECTIONS

1. Think about one thing you would really like to try doing but are afraid to fail at (*such as talking in front of your class, learning a new instrument, asking someone for a playdate, etc.*).

2. Write the best thing that could happen in the middle of the mind map on page 63 (*everyone listens to me, I am good at the instrument, the kid wants to play with me, etc.*).

3. Brainstorm all the possible things that could happen that keep you afraid of trying (*someone could laugh at you, etc.*). Then complete the mind map, including these possibilities by adding arrows and extra bubbles when needed.

4. Take a red marker and cross out all the fears that you can handle. Be brave, be bold!

What is the best thing
that can happen?

_____

MY GROWTH MINDSET TAKEAWAY

Completing this activity can make your mind calm. After you write
down everything that could go wrong and see that it's not so bad, it
makes it easier to try new things!

CHAPTER FIVE

I CAN KEEP TRYING!

Patchy Potatoes

Marco's aunt Rosa finally came to visit! Aunt Rosa decided to prepare her famous gnocchi with tomato sauce. Marco loves gnocchi, and he loves to cook with his aunt. So he quickly found a potato peeler and started to peel the potatoes while Aunt Rosa prepared the homemade tomato sauce.

After finishing two potatoes, Marco noticed that the potatoes still had some patches of peel left on them. *That's not good*, he thought to himself. He looked over at his aunt, but she seemed busy. So he kept peeling and peeling the same potato, and soon the potato nearly disappeared! If Marco kept going like that, there would not be enough potatoes left for the gnocchi!

"Aunt Rosa," he whispered. Busy with the tomato sauce, his aunt didn't hear him, so Marco tried again. "Aunt Rosa, how can I do this better?" Rosa turned to Marco to inspect his progress and smiled. "Oh, these little brown patches? You can just remove them with this little tool on top of the peeler. That should work fine. Now, can you hand me the salt?"

Try Again and Ask for Help

At first, Marco felt a little uncomfortable asking his aunt to help him with peeling the potatoes, but for Aunt Rosa it was no big deal and she was able to help. It was actually easy for Marco to ask his aunt for help. Now Marco knows how to get rid of those brown patches, and if his little sister is going to help out, Marco will be able to teach her how to do it!

Just as Marco learned, it is important to ask for help when you need it. Having a growth mindset means learning and improving over time. There is nothing bad about asking for help. People are usually more than happy to help you!

Yes, You Can Help Me!

Having a growth mindset doesn't mean that you have to do everything by yourself. You can learn a lot, and usually quicker, by asking for help at the right time. Asking for help can be hard or embarrassing at first, but once you do it, it's a relief! The first step in asking for help is accepting help. In this activity, we are going to practice asking for help by learning to accept help from others.

WHAT YOU NEED

- courage

DIRECTIONS

For one whole day, every single time someone you know offers you help, go ahead and accept it. Think about how getting that help makes you feel.

REMEMBER

"Don't be afraid to ask for help when you need it. I do that every day. Asking for help isn't a sign of weakness; it's a sign of strength. It shows you have the courage to admit when you don't know something, and to learn something new."

—**Barack Obama**, 44th President of the United States

MY GROWTH MINDSET TAKEAWAY

This activity will help you feel better about accepting help. After all, even Barack Obama asks for help when he needs it! By accepting help when it's offered to you, you'll be more confident asking for help!

Asking Doesn't Cost a Thing

This activity is best to complete after you've already completed activity 26: "Yes, You Can Help Me!"

Now we are going to take getting help a step further! You've already practiced accepting help; let's ask for help three different times.

WHAT YOU NEED

- courage

DIRECTIONS

1. Three times in one day, try to ask someone you know (a school friend, teacher, or someone in your family) for help with something.

2. Note your progress on the following lines. What did you need help with today? How did it go? Did you learn anything from the help?

_____

_____

_____

_____

_____

_____

REMEMBER

What you need help with does not have to be something big. Asking someone just to open your bottle of juice or to help with a homework problem is totally fine.

MY GROWTH MINDSET TAKEAWAY

This exercise improves our ability to ask for help. Asking for help when we need it makes us stronger and smarter!

My "Practice Makes Perfect" Mind Map

You know now that to get better at anything, you need to practice. We all do. Even pro ball players and famous singers need to practice!

WHAT YOU NEED

- a pencil or pen

DIRECTIONS

Think of some things that need to be practiced before they can be mastered. Add them to the mind map below. Feel free to add extra lines and bubbles of your own if you have more ideas.

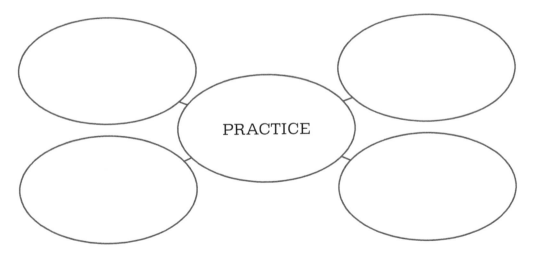

MY GROWTH MINDSET TAKEAWAY

The more we practice, the better we get, and now we know that everyone needs to practice if we want to stay at the top of our game!

FAIL: First Attempt in Learning

Many people think of failure as a bad thing, but it really means: *First **A**ttempt **In** Learning.* When we fail, we learn from it and keep practicing, and when we keep practicing, we do better!

DIRECTIONS

Think about a time when you failed at something, but later got better and finally were able to do it. How did it make you feel when you first tried and failed? How did you feel after accomplishing your goal?

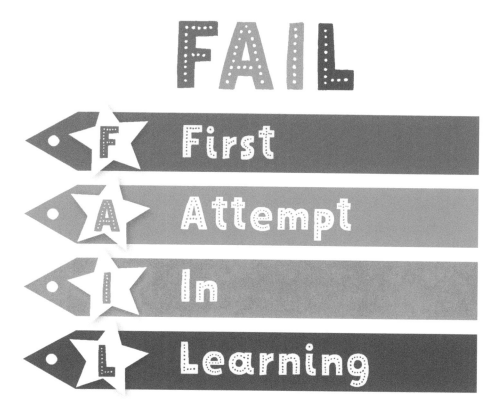

Get Better Every Time

Growth mindset thoughts focus on how you are going to do something. You might not be able to do that thing now, but that doesn't mean you will never be able to do it. Far from it—you can do anything! But you will sometimes need to put extra time and effort into things that are important to you. Remember that shifting from a fixed mindset is as easy as adding the little word "yet" on the end of a fixed mindset thought. You can go from "I can't do that" to "I can't do that, yet." This little-but-powerful word makes all the difference!

A growth mindset really works. Tell yourself: "With time and effort, I can improve!"

WHAT YOU NEED

- a timer (such as on a phone or a microwave)
- a simple puzzle (20 to 60 pieces)
- a pencil

DIRECTIONS

1. Choose a simple puzzle that you can finish in under 10 minutes. You are going to do this puzzle three times.
2. To start, put the pieces all to one side, start the timer, and try to finish as quickly as possible. Write your time in the time tracker on page 73. See if you can beat Josie's time!
3. Repeat step 2 twice more. How did your time improve?

Name	Time
Josie	10:02 minutes

MY GROWTH MINDSET TAKEAWAY

This exercise shows you how we usually improve with practice. The more time you put into completing the puzzle, the quicker you will become. Imagine how good you'd get if you did this puzzle every day for a week! The same is true with other things in your life, whether it's math, spelling, sports, music, art, or something else. The more often you practice, the better you will get!

Famous Folks Failed First!

Even though we sometimes hate failures, they're a part of life. We know that without failure, nothing could ever be created. To be able to create or do anything, we first need to be okay with failing.

WHAT YOU NEED

- help from an adult
- Internet access

DIRECTIONS

Pick one of the following famous people:

Walt Disney	Vera Wang	Soichiro Honda
Michael Jordan	Dwayne "the Rock" Johnson	Colonel Harland David Sanders
J. K. Rowling	Katy Perry	Pablo Picasso
Bill Gates	Lady Gaga	Taylor Swift
Theodor Geisel (Dr. Seuss)	Beyoncé Knowles	Katherine Johnson
Oprah Winfrey	Jay-Z	Claude Monet

- How did they fail?
- What did they learn from their mistakes?
- Did they give up?
- What can you learn from this person's failure?

MY GROWTH MINDSET TAKEAWAY

Be okay with failing! The first step in learning something is failing at something.

CHAPTER SIX

I CAN BE CREATIVE!

Tower Trouble

Mae's mother asked her how her day was, but Mae didn't hear anything. Her brother was not at home, so she was busy combining both of their Lego building blocks and was building the biggest tower ever!

The tower was already nearly as high as Mae, and it looked really cool. It had lots of windows, and Mae had even added a garage for her brother's toy cars. She already knew how the top of the tower would look, and she was excited to make it! Just as Mae put the last of the Legos on top of the tower, it started to wobble. She held on to the tower and tried to stabilize it, but it was too late. Everything crashed down to the floor.

What went wrong?

The tower looked great, and Mae was so close to finishing it. She stepped back to take a look at the entire building and decided that the tower probably was built too thin without the right support. If she used a stronger base, it would probably work! Quickly, she started to build the tower again.

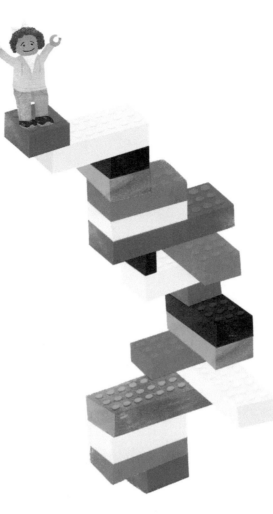

All Roads Lead to Rome

Ever heard of the saying "All roads lead to Rome"?

Rome was a very important city that was so well connected with other cities and villages in the Roman Empire that this saying started to appear. "All roads lead to Rome" means that no matter which road you choose, you will always be able to get back to Rome. In other words, you can get the same outcome by following many methods or ideas.

Bridge Challenge

As we just learned, there are many ways to reach the same outcome. "All roads lead to Rome," and some roads have bridges to help get us there. So let's build the strongest bridge we can, just with ice pop sticks and wood glue.

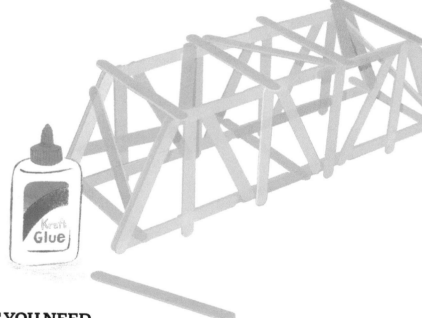

WHAT YOU NEED

- paper and a pencil
- ice pop sticks
- wood glue
- some small books

DIRECTIONS

1. Think about the design your bridge should have. Get inspired by the picture example on page 79, or come up with a completely new design of your own. Before you start building, draw what you think your bridge should look like.

2. Start building! Here's some advice: Before combining the sides of your bridge, first build each side separately. When gluing them together, make sure they're as straight as possible. A slight tilt will make the structure much weaker.

3. Wait until the glue on your bridge is completely dry. This step is important; otherwise, the bridge won't be strong.

4. Test your bridge. Place your bridge between some books or other objects to keep it sturdy. Now test the strength of your bridge by putting as many books on top of the bridge as it can hold before it collapses.

REMEMBER

You can achieve things in many different ways, but some ways work better than others. The good thing is that you can always practice and try again to improve.

MY GROWTH MINDSET TAKEAWAY

This is a fun and exciting activity! There are so many ways to build a strong bridge. This activity teaches us to be creative and look for different ways to solve a problem. This activity can be done several times, so go ahead and try—you can always improve your design. Maybe next time, instead of building the strongest bridge, you can build the most beautiful bridge? Or combine the most beautiful bridge with the strongest bridge?

What Would They Do?

Coming up with solutions to a problem can be hard. To help us think outside the box, we can pretend that we are someone else!

DIRECTIONS

1. Choose a person in your life who you respect and think is a good problem solver, such as an older brother or sister, parent, aunt or uncle, grandparent, teacher, or family friend. You can also choose from the list of famous people on page 74.

2. Now look at the following problems and approach each problem as if you are this person. What do you think they would do? How do you think they would handle it?

Problem 1: *You want to bake a cake, but you left the recipe at school. It's important that you finish the cake before tomorrow morning. What would* _____ *do?*

Problem 2: *You forgot that you have a spelling test tomorrow, and you really want to get a great mark on the test. You also told your friend that you would see them in the afternoon, but there won't be enough time to visit your friend and study for the spelling test. What would* _____ *do?*

Problem 3: *You got a 1,000-piece puzzle for your birthday. There are so many pieces that it took you five minutes to find any that fit together! You feel overwhelmed but also want to finish the puzzle. What would* _____ *do?*

Problem 4: *You tried all day yesterday to practice roller skating. Still, your friends are better than you, and that makes you feel kind of left out. What would _____ do?*

MY GROWTH MINDSET TAKEAWAY

In order to solve problems, we sometimes need to be creative and do things we normally would not think of. Taking the growth mindset of our most admired grown-up allows us to consider solutions we might not have thought of before.

Finish It Up

Sometimes you need to improvise when solving a problem. Improvising means you come up with an answer right in the moment, without preparing for it. You won't always get the chance to start and finish a problem all by yourself. Here, you'll finish a task that someone else started. Look at the drawings below and finish them. Be creative and make it fun!

WHAT YOU NEED

- a pencil or colored pencils

DIRECTIONS

Someone didn't finish their drawings! Try finishing the following drawings by using the lines they left.

MY GROWTH MINDSET TAKEAWAY

This activity is a great one to practice to become a flexible thinker and problem solver. Figuring out how to use the existing lines in your own drawing requires you to be creative and open-minded.

"In Honor of Books" Bookmarks

Let me tell you a secret: You can learn from the most amazing and most successful people in the world, even if you've never met them. It's true! Most people who have created something extraordinary want to share their knowledge with everyone. They spend hours and hours putting their knowledge into words and thinking about the best ways to introduce you to their area of expertise. Do you know what they do? They write books! It's amazing, if you think about it. Authors take time to write everything down for you to learn and digest. Having a growth mindset means always learning, and one way of learning is to learn from others. I really encourage you to use this gift!

So how can we use reading as a growth mindset lesson? Well, let's take your favorite growth mindset statement and put it on a bookmark! Books are amazing, and so are the people who write them. Read every day, and use your bookmark as a reminder of all the good knowledge you're feeding your brain!

WHAT YOU NEED

- felt-tip pens
- scissors
- construction paper

DIRECTIONS

1. Choose your favorite growth mindset quote or statement. Write the statement on the template (pattern) on page 87. Cut the template out and glue it on a piece of construction paper to make your bookmark stronger.

2. Add colors and maybe some cool new patterns on the back. Get inspired by the templates on page 86. Make it fun and be bold!

3. Anything can be a bookmark! When you run out of the templates, you can just draw and cut the shape of a bookmark out of your construction paper.

Some growth mindset statement examples:

- "I can't do that, *yet*!"
- "I'm going to practice to become a _____!"
- "Mistakes help me grow."
- "I can do hard things."
- "I can try new things."
- "I'm an epic problem solver."
- "I can train my brain."
- "I never give up!"

MY GROWTH MINDSET TAKEAWAY

Books are an amazing way of learning from others and embracing a growth mindset. Our mindset gets bigger when we build upon the knowledge and findings of others, and books are an awesome way of learning about them. Use your brand-new bookmark as a reminder of how you're always learning new things!

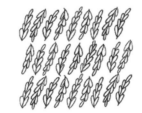

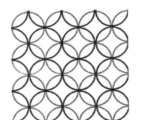

Lego Boat Power

Let's have some fun solving a problem. We need to build a boat out of Lego bricks to transport as many coins as possible. How can we do that without the boat sinking? We'll see!

WHAT YOU NEED

- paper
- pen
- Legos
- a container with water (bowl, sink, or bathtub)
- coins

DIRECTIONS

1. Think about a cool design for your Lego boat. Make a quick sketch on a piece of paper. Build your boat, and try to stick to your design as closely as possible.

2. Put the boat to the test and see if it floats on the water. Now, one at a time, add as many coins as you can on the boat until it sinks.

3. Count the number of coins your first boat was able to hold, and write it down. Now make changes to the design until your boat can hold at least twice the number of coins as your original boat!

My first boat held _____ *coins before it sunk.*

My best design can hold _____ *coins before it sinks.*

MY GROWTH MINDSET TAKEAWAY

It's exciting to see how your design improves over time. Your Lego boat got much better, and while practicing and getting better, you saw that you can also have fun!

Crazy Can Be Good!

It's not always easy to know the right way to approach a problem. One good way of getting ideas for how to solve a problem is to brainstorm, or think about it and come up with ideas. Unfortunately, we sometimes label our ideas as stupid or dumb, and this limits our creativity and our possible solutions. But funny, crazy ideas are sometimes the best!

WHAT YOU NEED

- a pencil
- an open mind

DIRECTIONS

1. Look at the problems described on pages 92–93 and make a list of the absolute dumbest, funniest, or craziest possible solutions to the problem you can think of. Don't judge or limit your ideas—go ahead and write them.

2. Now look at your long list of solutions and circle those that might not be as dumb or ridiculous as you originally thought!

Problem 1: *You forgot your gym clothes.*

_____

_____

_____

_____

Problem 2: *Your umbrella broke in the middle of a rain shower.*

_____

_____

_____

_____

Problem 3: *Come up with a problem of your own.*

_____

_____

_____

_____

MY GROWTH MINDSET TAKEAWAY

This activity helps with instant problem solving. Sometimes we get stuck and don't know how to start thinking about solutions. Thinking about strange, dumb ways of solving a problem can lead to wonderful, clever ideas!

CHAPTER SEVEN

I CAN TRY NEW THINGS!

New Game, Same Alan

Alan has a sleepover with his cousin Ben this weekend. Ben is a little older than Alan and has so much cool stuff. The coolest thing is Ben's bunk bed, and for the sleepover, Alan is invited to sleep on the top bunk. Ben also has all the video games that you can imagine. When Alan arrives at the sleepover, Ben announces he has a new game he wants to try out today. Alan has heard a lot about this game in school, but he has never played it before. Starting new games always frightens Alan, and he likes to try them out alone at home so nobody can see how bad he is. Ben is way too excited to show Alan the game, so Alan uses all of his bravery and takes the controller. Suddenly, he is kind of excited and determined to have fun!

New Experiences, New Mistakes

New experiences can be scary. We are not sure what to expect, and there is a big chance that we will make mistakes. Things rarely work perfectly the first time we do them, but we also know how important mistakes are. They allow us to learn and grow!

Perfectly Imperfect

The best way to learn from our mistakes is to embrace them and be okay with failure. Each mistake we make is a chance to learn and grow! Trying to do things perfectly is actually the enemy of progress and learning!

For this activity, let's make things purposely not perfect!

DIRECTIONS

Answer the following questions incorrectly:

What's the capital of the country you live in?

How many people live on your street?

In which month is your birthday?

How many seasons are in a year?

What's your favorite animal?

What is 500 – 300 + 2?

How hard was it to answer these questions wrong?

REMEMBER

No one is perfect—that's why pencils have erasers!

MY GROWTH MINDSET TAKEAWAY

When people want to be perfect, they might develop negative self-talk (tell themselves they can't do something because they might make a mistake). They might also try to avoid challenging tasks, but these are the best kinds of tasks to help you learn and grow. Kids with a growth mindset know that mistakes are an opportunity to learn, and they understand that the effort is more important than the final result.

Taking Feedback

Receiving feedback is a great way of improving and learning, but it can also be hard because it can make you feel like you are being criticized. Practicing asking for feedback from people who love you is a great way of focusing on the helpful parts of feedback.

WHAT YOU NEED

- paper and a pencil
- a friend or family member who is willing to give you feedback

DIRECTIONS

1. Think about something you want to improve at, and write it down.
2. Think about a person who knows more about this skill than you do. Maybe this person is your parent or a friend. Write down their name.
3. Ask that person for feedback on how they think you could improve in this area. Do not respond, even if you disagree. Just listen and write the feedback down.
4. Thank them for their feedback!

MY GROWTH MINDSET TAKEAWAY

"We all need people that give us feedback. That's how we improve."

—**Bill Gates**, co-founder of Microsoft

I Can Empower Myself

In this chapter, we focus on being okay with mistakes and being brave enough to try new things. Each mistake is an opportunity to learn. But always having a positive outlook and embracing each mistake can be hard, sometimes very hard! When we start something new, the fear of failure can be scary. When you start to feel fixed mindset thoughts like "I can't do that" creeping up on you, it's good to have some tricks up your sleeve to overcome them.

DIRECTIONS

Let's try out a few things you can do the next time fixed mindset thoughts hold you back.

1. For 60 seconds, close your eyes and just listen to the sounds around you. What can you hear? Listen to the loud sounds first, and then try to notice as many sounds as possible. Can you hear your own heartbeat? Or your breath?
2. Think of a reward you can give yourself when you overcome your challenging new task.
3. Try "belly breathing" for 10 deep breaths. Breathe in as much as you can, and then breathe out as slowly as you can.

Which strategy works the best for you?

MY GROWTH MINDSET TAKEAWAY

It's okay to be afraid to try new things. What matters is what you do about it. The next time you feel nervous about trying something new, use your new strategies to empower you—you got this!

Overcome the Obstacle

Obstacles can appear when you try out new things. But you can also find obstacles when you're doing things that you've done many times before. Suddenly, something is different. For example, you need to run a race with new shoes that don't fit that well; on the day of the spelling test, you feel a little sick; or instead of working with your best friend, your teacher pairs you up with someone new. All these things can be obstacles and can make the task a little harder. Harder, but not impossible!

WHAT YOU NEED

- a pencil

DIRECTIONS

For this activity, your job is to trace the lines on page 101. This may look easy, but you have one obstacle to overcome: Trace the lines by using the hand opposite from the one you usually write with!

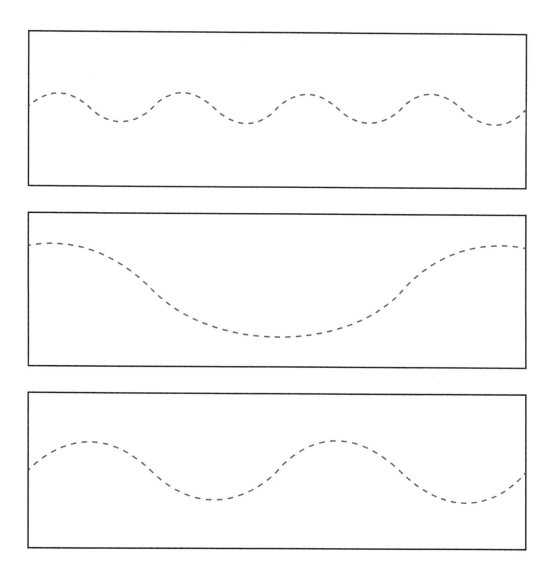

MY GROWTH MINDSET TAKEAWAY

You might be surprised at how much harder it is to do the same task with just a small obstacle in the way. But guess what. If you did this task every day, you would train your brain to be able to trace the lines better and better, even with your less-used hand! You are training your brain as if it were a muscle.

Challenges in the Chapters

The way we respond to obstacles can make the difference between failure and success!

WHAT YOU NEED

- a book with a growth mindset character
- paper and a pencil or pen

DIRECTIONS

Find a book in which the main character needs to overcome a challenge. The book should have a main character who shows a growth mindset. If you can't find a book like this, ask a parent, teacher, or librarian to help you find one. Once you find your book, answer the following questions:

- What's the main character's challenge?
- How did the person/character first respond when finding out about the challenge?
- When did the character show a growth mindset? Write down a sentence they said or an action they did that shows how they responded to the challenge.
- Draw a picture of the moment when they overcame the challenge.

MY GROWTH MINDSET TAKEAWAY

Books are an awesome way to experience different mindsets. By reading books, we can learn from others' mistakes and experiences without having to go through them ourselves.

Thanks for the Feedback!

Sometimes our friends see things from a different perspective, and this can help us improve. When we receive helpful feedback and know how to use that feedback to improve, it opens new doors for learning and growth.

WHAT YOU NEED

- paper and a pencil or pen

DIRECTIONS

1. Think of a time when you got really helpful feedback or advice from someone. Perhaps that feedback helped you improve or even complete a challenge. Write down who gave you that feedback, what it was about, and how it helped you improve or complete your challenge.

   - Who gave it?
   - What was it?
   - How did it help?

2. Write a short thank-you note for that person and give it to them.

   Example: Hi, Jody, I want to thank you for telling me how to hold the tennis racket in a different way. It was hard at first to change my way of holding the racket, but now I can see that the new way of holding it gives me more power when I hit the tennis ball. Thanks for giving me helpful feedback.

REMEMBER

Thinking of a time you received amazing, helpful feedback might take some time. Maybe you'll even get some good feedback today!

MY GROWTH MINDSET TAKEAWAY

Researchers have studied the effects of being grateful and found out that people who are regularly grateful and think about all the good things that happen to them are happier in life. So this activity does lots of things: It encourages your friend to continue giving you helpful feedback, it helps you grow, and it makes you happier!
So if you want, do this exercise once a week and see how it feels!

CHAPTER EIGHT

I CAN DREAM BIG!

All the Fish

Zahara is in elementary school, but she already knows that she wants to be a marine biologist when she grows up. She's known this since the first time she visited her cousin Marianne at her job.

Marianne knows so much about the ocean and all the creatures that live in it. Right now, Marianne is working on making the ocean a better place to live for turtles. "Becoming a marine biologist takes a long time," Marianne explained to Zahara when she visited, "and one needs to learn about all the animals in order to understand the complex ecosystems of the ocean."

Ever since that day, Zahara reads all the books she can find in her library about fish and the ocean. Last week, Zahara's class went to the local aquarium. She excitedly read all the plaques on the walls of every exhibit and asked lots of questions. She was able to learn so much!

What's Your Goal?

It's important to have goals. By having a goal, you can learn to make decisions that will help you reach it. Zahara knows that she wants to be a marine biologist, and she works toward her goal almost every day by learning about and studying the ocean.

In this chapter, we'll focus on figuring out your own goals and learning how to achieve them—all with the help of your growth mindset!

I'm Full of Goals

Did you know that people who write down their goals are much more likely to achieve them? You can turn a dream into a goal by simply writing it down!

WHAT YOU NEED

- colored pencils

DIRECTIONS

1. Fill in the circles with your 16 most important dreams or goals that you would love to achieve for today, next week, next year, or even 10 years from now (for example: getting 100 percent on a spelling test, playing an instrument, learning a new song for the piano, becoming a heart surgeon, etc.).

2. Now, which are your top three most important goals from the list? Once you decide, color them. These three goals should be your main focus.

REMEMBER

"If you have a goal, write it down. If you do not write it down, you do not have a goal—you have a wish."

—**Steve Maraboli**, speaker and author

MY GROWTH MINDSET TAKEAWAY

You just figured out your three most important goals—congratulations! Being aware of your goals is a big step. Keep them in mind throughout each day and try to make decisions that bring you closer to achieving these goals. Look for opportunities to learn more about these things!

I'm SMART and My Goals Are, Too

Not all goals are created equal. Goals are personal to you, so only YOU can decide if a goal is a good goal or a bad goal. But no matter what, your goals should be SMART! That means they should be:

S – Specific What EXACTLY are you trying to achieve?

M – Measurable How will you know you achieved your goal?

A – Achievable Your goal needs to be something you can achieve with time and effort.

R – Relevant Is this goal worth working hard to accomplish?

T – Timely What is your deadline to accomplish this goal?

WHAT YOU NEED

- a pencil

DIRECTIONS

Decide if the following goals are Specific, Measurable, Achievable, Relevant, and Timely (or SMART!).

GOAL	SPECIFIC	NOT SPECIFIC
"I want to read more."		
"I want to get a good grade in math."		
"I want to get 100 percent on a spelling test."		

GOAL	MEASURABLE	NOT MEASURABLE
"I want to run a mile in under one minute."		
"I want to be a good soccer player."		
"I want to become a teacher."		

GOAL	ACHIEVABLE	NOT ACHIEVABLE
"I want to read all the *Harry Potter* books in one night."		
"I want to clean my room every day."		
"I want to brush my teeth twice a day."		

GOAL	RELEVANT	NOT RELEVANT
"I want to finish the new puzzle."		
"I want to draw all the dog breeds that I know."		
"I want to read for 20 minutes every night."		

GOAL	TIMELY	NOT TIMELY
"I want to learn to cook an egg."		
"I want to finish my homework before dinner every day."		
"I want to meet up with my friends."		

Now put it all together!

GOAL	HAS ALL THE PARTS OF A SMART GOAL	DOES NOT HAVE ALL THE PARTS OF A SMART GOAL
"I want to finish my new book by the end of the school year."		
"I want to spend no more than 30 minutes on screen time every day, starting today."		
"I want to have more friends."		

MY GROWTH MINDSET TAKEAWAY

Now you understand what a SMART goal is! Having SMART goals will help you know they can be achieved.

SMART Goal Test Drive

In the last activity, you learned how to decide whether a goal is SMART or not. In this exercise, we are going to create your very own SMART goals.

WHAT YOU NEED

- a pencil

DIRECTIONS

Think about the goals you wrote down in activity 44: "I'm Full of Goals," and turn them into SMART goals. Pick one goal, and then say out loud how the goal can be a SMART goal.

Using your **top three goals**, fill out the following boards.

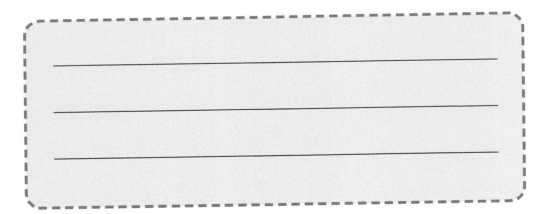

REMEMBER

If one or more of your top three goals cannot be SMART, you can choose a different one. For example, if your goal was to be able to fly by age 25, then that would fail the A for Achievable in the SMART requirement, because it's impossible for humans to fly on our own! You could decide to change your goal to "I want to become an airplane pilot by age 25." Or you could decide that your goal is not really Relevant—meaning it's not a goal worth working hard for—and choose a different one instead.

MY GROWTH MINDSET TAKEAWAY

Having your goal in the SMART format will help you come up with a plan to achieve it!

How to WOOP My Goals

Now that you have a list with your three great SMART goals, you can be proud of yourself. Just by writing down your goals, you are already halfway to achieving them. Good job! But now we need to come up with a plan for how to achieve your goals. We will use the WOOP method, a helpful tool that is easy to remember.

Step 1: *W – Wish*

Step 2: *O – Outcome*

Step 3: *O – Obstacles*

Step 4: *P – Plan*

WHAT YOU NEED

- paper and a pencil
- your imagination
- a partner (optional)

DIRECTIONS

1. W stands for Wish.
   Your wish is one of your SMART goals from the previous exercise. Choose one and write that goal down.

2. O stands for Outcome.
   Now comes the best part. Imagine that you already achieved your goal. How does it feel? How do you feel different? Feel how proud you are. Take your time with this step.
   (If you have a hard time imagining this in your head, you can also do this step with a partner. Talk with your partner about how you imagined you achieved your goal and how it feels.)

3. O stands for Obstacles.

   Write down all the possible obstacles that could get in the way of achieving your goal. These could even be feelings or thoughts that prevent you from achieving them.

4. P stands for Plan.

   Now we'll create a plan for the main obstacle you just discovered by using the following formula: "If [obstacle] happens, then I will [action]." This way, if you are faced with that obstacle in real life, you'll already know what to do to get through it!

5. Repeat the WOOP activity for all three of your chosen goals!

Wish: _____

Outcome: _____

Obstacles: _____

Plan: _____

Wish: _____

Outcome: _____

Obstacles: _____

Plan: _____

Wish: _____

Outcome: _____

Obstacles: _____

Plan: _____

MY GROWTH MINDSET TAKEAWAY

Making a plan to achieve your goals increases your chances to achieve those goals. Congratulations—you are rocking it!

Activity 48

Sharing My Plans

Now you have three exciting goals and a plan for how to achieve them! One more thing you can do to increase the chances of achieving your goals? Tell other people about them!

Telling others about your goals will make you more motivated, since you'll probably want to stick to what you told them.

WHAT YOU NEED

- a partner

DIRECTIONS

Choose someone you trust and tell them about your top three goals. If you'd like, you can also tell them about the potential obstacles you've already thought about and the plan you came up with that you will follow once you are facing these obstacles. (They may even have some valuable feedback for you!)

MY GROWTH MINDSET TAKEAWAY

Now that you shared with others that you are going to learn the piano, for example, people will check in with you to see how well you're doing! Because of this, you will feel obligated to yourself and to others to stick to the goals you said you would achieve. This is a good thing!

A Token Reminder

We know that having goals is an important step toward achieving them. But another step is to remember your goals on a daily basis. Thinking about your goals will help you keep making progress toward reaching them.

WHAT YOU NEED

- a token of your choice (see directions)

DIRECTIONS

Take your top goal and think about a token that can remind you of your goal. Your token can be anything, but it's best to choose something that can easily be carried along. Some good ideas are a beautiful stone you found outdoors, a necklace, a chestnut from the forest, or even your favorite Lego figure. Keep this token with you at all times until you reach your goal.

MY GROWTH MINDSET TAKEAWAY

Choosing and keeping an item with you to remind you of your goals is a great way to stay motivated and always remind you of what you are trying to achieve.

CHAPTER NINE

I CAN KEEP GOING!

Chef on the Rise

Dylan's biggest wish is to be a chef in a fancy restaurant in New York City. He finds himself daydreaming about what his kitchen would look like and how he would receive five-star reviews on the Internet. *My restaurant will be so good*, he thinks, *people will have to make reservations months in advance.*

For now, Dylan tries out new recipes together with his dad. They've already made some tasty salads with tomato and cucumbers, and even complicated sandwiches that are so tall they're hard to bite.

Dylan likes to follow recipes, but he also loves to experiment with new flavors. His newest project is to find a way to make celery taste delicious. A few times, though, his creations haven't turned out up to his own high standard. Peanut butter roast beef sandwiches are not as good as he imagined! And one day, he forgot to add baking soda into the recipe for his mom's favorite pancakes, and they came out flat and rubbery. Not even the cat would eat them! More determined than ever, he never stops trying. In fact, the next time he made pancakes, they were perfect. He never forgot the baking soda again.

Be Like Dylan: Embrace a Growth Mindset

Dylan knows that he can always try again, and each time he tries, he either learns how to improve his amazing creations or he makes something tasty! Dylan has a total growth mindset. He loves to learn, practice, and improve. And mistakes don't hold him back— they help him get better. Be like Dylan!

Mindset Matchup

There are so many things you can take away from all the activities you've already completed in this book. One big one is the importance of practicing and repetition. Let's look at the sentences below and embrace our growth mindset!

WHAT YOU NEED

- a pencil
- a partner

DIRECTIONS

1. Circle the correct answer for a growth mindset.
2. Can you think of situations when your inner voice told you one of these things? Talk about it with your partner.

- "I can (always/never) learn."
- "Mistakes make (my pain/my brain) grow."
- "Things are difficult (before they are easy/so I better not try)."
- "Mistakes are a part of (learning/failures)."
- "My goal is (perfection/progress)."
- "Struggling makes me (stronger/weak)."
- "I am (intimidated/inspired) by the success of others."
- "I can ask for (solutions/help) when I need it."

MY GROWTH MINDSET TAKEAWAY

Switching from a fixed mindset to a growth mindset can be hard. It's important to never stop learning and keep reminding yourself about the differences between these two mindsets and where each of them will take you. As you finish this book, keep practicing to identify the different ways of looking at the same situation. This will keep you improving and growing!

All the Things I've Learned

It's super helpful to make connections between the concepts you have learned and experiences in your life.

WHAT YOU NEED

* a partner

DIRECTIONS

Think back to the last couple of weeks. With a partner, take turns talking about an experience you had that relates to the following ideas:

* *The brain is a muscle*
* *Accepting and giving helpful feedback*
* *The power of the small word "yet"*
* *Overcoming challenges and obstacles*
* *Trying hard*
* *Not giving up*
* *Overcoming negative self-talk*
* *Dealing with mistakes*
* *Choosing goals and working toward them*

MY GROWTH MINDSET TAKEAWAY

Just knowing about the growth mindset is not enough—it's important to use it and live by it, too! This activity will help you see where and when you have already been able to follow a growth mindset!

My Promises to Myself

In this activity, you are going to make some promises to yourself. This way, you're making a commitment to keep following the growth mindset ideas that you learned and practiced throughout this book.

WHAT YOU NEED

- a pencil

DIRECTIONS

Look at the promises below and sign off on them to promise yourself that you will *keep* your promises. At the end, you will find two empty lines. Come up with your own growth mindset promises to yourself!

I will follow my goals!   Sign here: _____
Even when things are hard, I will stick to my goals.

I'm not giving up!   Sign here: _____
When I feel like giving up, I promise myself I will keep trying.

I welcome helpful feedback!   Sign here: _____
When I receive feedback, I will take a deep breath and try to learn from it.

Mistakes are my friends!   Sign here: _____
When I make mistakes, I know I'm learning.

_____   Sign here: _____

_____   Sign here: _____

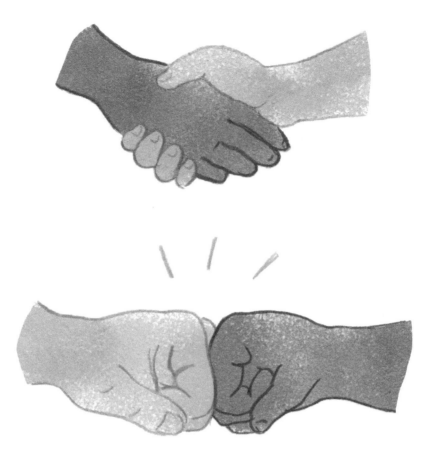

REMEMBER

"Becoming is better than being."

—**Carol S. Dweck**, psychologist and growth mindset researcher

GROWTH MINDSET TAKEAWAY

Try to stick to your promises. You can always come back to this page and check to see if you are keeping them. Don't get discouraged if you forget to keep your promises once or twice! What matters is that you keep your promises *most* of the time. Part of having a growth mindset means that you can make mistakes and keep practicing to get better.

Activity 53

I'm Proud of My Progress

By coming this far, you've really shown that you embrace a growth mindset! There are a lot of activities in this book, so it would have been easy to just give up and not do them, but you kept going. Congratulations!

WHAT YOU NEED

- a partner

DIRECTIONS

In this activity, think about the activities you completed in this book and talk about them with a partner.

1. Which activities are you most proud of?
2. Think about an activity that seemed hard at first, but you managed to finish it. How did finishing it make you feel?
3. Which activity was the most fun?

Now decide on an activity you want to do again, and go for it!

MY GROWTH MINDSET TAKEAWAY

Thinking about your accomplishments is a great way to keep going! Take some time to be grateful for what you are already good at and all the things you can already accomplish.

I Remember This!

By reading this book and completing the activities, you've learned a ton about growth mindset concepts. Awesome work!

WHAT YOU NEED

- a pencil or pen

DIRECTIONS

Write down a couple of the concepts, sayings, or ideas that stuck with you the most and that you want to remember. What do you think caused these things to stick with you?

_____

_____

_____

_____

_____

_____

_____

_____

REMEMBER

Take your time, and know that you can always flick through this book again to spark your memory and remind yourself of what it takes to keep on growing!

MY GROWTH MINDSET TAKEAWAY

This is an important activity, because it challenges you to think about all the great things you learned and choose your favorite. Take your time and think deeply about which concepts you want to remember and use more often in your daily life from now on.

What's My Mindset NOW?

You probably remember this activity from the beginning of the book. Don't look back at it yet. Just go through the same list of statements and see how much you've already improved!

WHAT YOU NEED

- markers or colored pencils

DIRECTIONS

1. Look at the following statements and color the face that shows best how you feel about this statement.
2. Add all your points to receive your final score.

STATEMENTS	AGREE - NOT SURE - DISAGREE
"When something is hard, I want to work on it more."	🙂 😐 🙁
"I can always improve, so I keep trying."	🙂 😐 🙁
"I can train my brain."	🙂 😐 🙁
"I have no problem making mistakes."	🙂 😐 🙁
"It's okay when things don't work for me right away."	🙂 😐 🙁

"I love seeing others succeed."	🙂	😐	🙁
"I can get smarter when I work hard."	🙂	😐	🙁
"Mistakes help me learn better."	🙂	😐	🙁
"I can learn anything I want to."	🙂	😐	🙁
"I like to learn new things even when I make mistakes."	🙂	😐	🙁

Number of 🙁 : _____

Number of 😐 : _____

Number of 🙂 : _____

Give yourself 1 point for each 🙁 , 2 points for each 😐 ,

and 3 points for each 🙂 .

Growth Mindset points: _____

GROWTH MINDSET EXPERT (24–30 POINTS)	You are a true Growth Mindset Expert! You know that the right mindset helps you achieve your goals and dreams. When it gets hard, you overcome negative self-talk and embrace a growth mindset. Great job! You also know how important practice and repetition are for a growth mindset. Your hard work and effort paid off! Keep it going!
GROWTH MINDSET WARRIOR (17–23 POINTS)	You're a Growth Mindset Warrior! You did a great job. You have growth mindset ideas in your head and follow them most of the time. I love it! You can go through your favorite exercises again to keep learning and improving. You're not far off from becoming a Growth Mindset Expert!
GROWTH MINDSET STARTER (10–16 POINTS)	You are a Growth Mindset Starter! You've learned a lot, but keep going over some of the activities again to keep learning how to embrace a growth mindset and make it stronger all the time. Remember, by continuing to practice, you will always improve!

MY GROWTH MINDSET TAKEAWAY

The goal is not to always have a growth mindset. The goal is to notice when fixed mindset thoughts are getting in the way of accomplishing your goals. Whenever you notice you have fixed mindset thoughts, take a deep breath and see if you can change your thinking.

This book gave you a lot of tools and tricks that you can use to help you. The real test will be using these tools to practice having growth mindset thoughts, especially with the opportunities you will have every day. You can choose to follow a growth mindset every day. Keep practicing, keep improving, keep growing, and keep chasing your dreams! You are amazing and can achieve great things!

Resources for Kids

BOOKS

Growth Mindset Series: *A World without Failures* by Esther Pia Cordova

> *What would a world without mistakes look like? Join David in this picture book and discover that it might not be as exciting as once thought.*

Growth Mindset Series: *I Can't Do That, YET* by Esther Pia Cordova

> *You can achieve so many things through hard work and by having the right mindset. This picture book focuses on the powerful word "yet." Maybe you can't do something, but that only means you can't do something, YET!*

Growth Mindset Series: *Your Thoughts Matter* by Esther Pia Cordova

> *A picture book that shows the two different mindsets as imaginary friends Growi and Fixi. A great story that will make you think about your own inner voices. What do your own Growi and Fixi look like?*

Mistakes That Worked: 40 Familiar Inventions & How They Came to Be by Charlotte Foltz Jones

> *A collection of funny accidents that led to some awesome results! Best read with a parent so you can discuss the inventions that look familiar to you.*

Your Fantastic Elastic Brain: Stretch It, Shape It by JoAnn Deak, PhD

> *A picture book that explains how your brain works and what you can do to help it achieve wonderful things.*

Resources for Grown-Ups

BOOKS

Mindset: The New Psychology of Success by Carol S. Dweck, PhD

> *Start here! Dr. Carol S. Dweck's research jump-started the conversation about the concept of different mindsets and how they can affect our children. It's a deep dive into the research and background of growth mindset.*

In Other Words: Phrases for Growth Mindset: A Teacher's Guide to Empowering Students through Effective Praise and Feedback by Annie Brock and Heather Hundley

> *This is a great resource for practical advice on what to say to your child in order to foster a growth mindset. There are many great examples to choose from.*

The Growth Mindset Coach: A Teacher's Month-by-Month Handbook for Empowering Students to Achieve by Annie Brock and Heather Hundley

> *Especially helpful for teachers and counselors who are looking to have a structured plan on how to introduce growth mindset in their classroom. Great hands-on lesson plans and real-life educator stories are included!*

Mindsets in the Classroom: Building a Culture of Success and Student Achievement in Schools by Mary Cay Ricci

> *Another great tool for teachers, with the focus on building a growth mindset culture in school. This book is very detailed and practical for the classroom.*

Talent Is Overrated: What Really Separates World-Class

Performers from Everybody Else by Geoff Colvin

> *What makes world-class performers so remarkable? This book lists principles of great performance backed up with scientific research and offers practical advice on how to achieve better results without relying on talent or hard work exclusively.*

The Talent Code: Greatness Isn't Born. It's Grown. Here's How. by Daniel Coyle

> *This book looks at growth mindset from the perspective of how the brain mechanism works when following growth mindset habits. Plenty of examples are included to show how regular people achieved outstanding results, which are very empowering and motivate readers to follow the book's advice.*

Grit: The Power of Passion and Perseverance by Angela Duckworth

> *This book will show you that your mindset has a much bigger impact on your results than your talent or luck.*

WEBSITES

PowerOfYet.com

> *This is my website, containing more information and resources on the subject of growth mindset.*

ClassDojo: The Mojo Show: ideas.ClassDojo.com/b/growth-mindset

> *Meet Mojo, who recently discovered the concepts of a growth mindset. Watch these short and fun videos to get an additional summary of what a growth mindset is and what it can do for you.*

References

Associated Press. "Science Watch; Inch by Inch to the Moon." *New York Times*. December 23, 1997. NYTimes.com/1997 /12/23/science/science-watch-inch-by-inch-to-the-moon.html.

Blackwell, Lisa S., Kali H. Trzesniewski, and Carol S. Dweck. "Implicit Theories of Intelligence Predict Achievement Across an Adolescent Transition: A Longitudinal Study and an Intervention." *Child Development* 78, no. 1 (February 28, 2007): 246–63. doi:10.1111 /j.1467-8624.2007.00995.x.

Clabaugh, Jeff. "Hot Dogs Still Reign Supreme at MLB Ballparks." WTOP News. March 28, 2019. WTOP.com/business-finance /2019/03/hot-dogs-still-reign-supreme-at-mlb-ballparks.

Dweck, Carol S. *Mindset: The New Psychology of Success*. New York: Ballantine Books, 2007.

Gates, Bill. "Teachers Need Real Feedback." Filmed April 2013. TED video, 10:09. TED.com/talks/bill_gates_teachers_need_real _feedback#t-6992.

Goldman, Robert, and Stephen Papson. *Nike Culture: The Sign of the Swoosh*. London: SAGE Publications Ltd, 1998.

Maraboli, Steve. *Unapologetically You: Reflections on Life and the Human Experience*. Port Washington, NY: A Better Today Publishing, 2013.

Obama, Barack. "Remarks by the President in a National Address to America's Schoolchildren." The White House. September 8, 2009. Accessed 2/20/2020. ObamaWhiteHouse. Archives.gov/the-press-office/remarks-president-a-national-address-americas-schoolchildren.

Reference. "How Many Grains of Rice Are in a Pound?" Accessed February 18, 2020. Reference.com/world-view/many-grains-rice-pound-cda73bedba89ff9b.

World Atlas. "How Many Cats Are There in the World?" Accessed February 20, 2020. WorldAtlas.com/articles/how-many-cats-are-there-in-the-world.html.

World Atlas. "How Many Dogs Are There in the World?" Accessed February 20, 2020. WorldAtlas.com/articles/how-many-dogs-are-there-in-the-world.html.

US Census Bureau. "US and World Population Clock." Accessed February 20, 2020. Census.gov/popclock.

Yanev, Victor. "Video Game Demographics: Who Plays Games in 2020." TechJury. May 2, 2019. TechJury.net/stats-about/video-game-demographics.

Zorn, Eric. "Without Failure, Jordan Would Be False Idol." *Chicago Tribune*. May 19, 1997. ChicagoTribune.com/news/ct-xpm-1997-05-19-9705190096-story.html.

Zuckerman, Catherine. "The Human Brain, Explained." *National Geographic*. October 15, 2009. NationalGeographic.com/science/health-and-human-body/human-body/brain/#close.

Answer Key

CHAPTER ONE

ACTIVITY 2: WATER MY THOUGHTS

- ~~"I'm bad. I give up."~~
- "It's going to take some time and effort."
- ~~"I will never be able to read well."~~
- ~~"It's impossible."~~
- "I made a mistake, but next time I will do it better."
- "I can't do it, YET."
- ~~"This is too hard."~~
- "I'm getting a little better every day."

ACTIVITY 3: POSITIVE OR NEGATIVE SELF-TALK?

SELF-TALK SENTENCES	GROWTH MINDSET	FIXED MINDSET
1. "I can't do this because I'm dumb."		X
2. "I did a great job."	X	
3. "This is difficult, but I can kind of do it."	X	
4. "I can't do this, yet."	X	
5. "I am proud of myself."	X	
6. "They don't want to be my friend because I'm stupid."		X
7. "I'm the worst ever."		X
8. "I hate this."		X
9. "My friend is so good at math, but with practice I will be, too."	X	
10. "I'm no good at this."		X
11. "I will never get that right!"		X
12. "I will keep trying."	X	
13. "I love this challenge!"	X	
14. "One day, I will be able to do it."	X	
15. "Everyone will think I'm crazy."		X

16.	"It's not good yet, but I will spend more time improving."	X	
17.	"I am so ugly."		X
18.	"My head hurts from thinking hard, but I can see the progress I made."	X	
19.	"I am so stupid."		X
20.	"This is hard, but with practice I can do it."	X	

ACTIVITY 6: SPOT THE MINDSET

Fixed Mindset

Growth Mindset

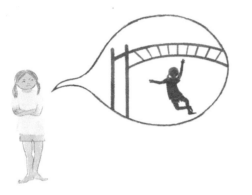

CHAPTER TWO

ACTIVITY 8: BRAIN TOUR

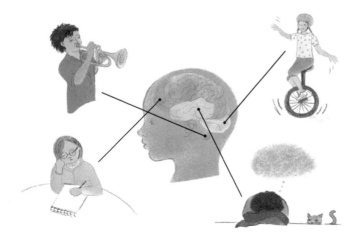

ACTIVITY 10: WHAT'S GOOD FOR MY BRAIN?

ACTIVITY 13: COLOR MY BRAIN

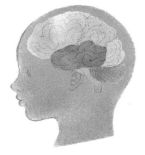

CHAPTER THREE

ACTIVITY 16: A WORLD WITHOUT MISTAKES

ITEM	WOULD NOT EXIST	WOULD EXIST
apples		X
clothes	X	
phones	X	
supermarkets	X	
stones		X
houses	X	
electricity	X	
the sun		X

glasses	X	
refrigerators	X	
Internet	X	

ACTIVITY 18: HELPFUL FEEDBACK VS. UNHELPFUL FEEDBACK

CHAPTER EIGHT

ACTIVITY 45: I'M SMART AND MY GOALS ARE, TOO

GOAL	SPECIFIC	NOT SPECIFIC
"I want to read more."		X
"I want to get a good grade in math."		X
"I want to get 100 percent on a spelling test."	X	

GOAL	MEASURABLE	NOT MEASURABLE
"I want to run a mile in under one minute."	X	
"I want to be a good soccer player."		X
"I want to become a teacher."		X

GOAL	ACHIEVABLE	NOT ACHIEVABLE
"I want to read all the *Harry Potter* books in one night."		X
"I want to clean my room every day."	X	
"I want to brush my teeth twice a day."	X	

GOAL	RELEVANT	NOT RELEVANT
"I want to finish the new puzzle."	X	
"I want to draw all the dog breeds that I know."		X
"I want to read for 20 minutes every night."	X	

GOAL	TIMELY	NOT TIMELY
"I want to learn to cook an egg."		X
"I want to finish my homework before dinner every day."	X	
"I want to meet up with my friends."		X

Now put it all together!

GOAL	HAS ALL THE PARTS OF A SMART GOAL	DOES NOT HAVE ALL THE PARTS OF A SMART GOAL
"I want to finish my new book by the end of the school year."	X	
"I want to spend no more than 30 minutes on screen time every day, starting today."	X	
"I want to have more friends."		X

CHAPTER NINE

ACTIVITY 50: MINDSET MATCHUP

- "I can (always)/never) learn."
- "Mistakes make (my pain/(my brain) grow."
- "Things are difficult (before they are easy)/so I better not try)."
- "Mistakes are a part of (learning)/failures)."
- "My goal is (perfection/(progress))."
- "Struggling makes me (stronger)/weak)."
- "I am (intimidated/(inspired) by the success of others."
- "I can ask for (solutions/(help) when I need it."

About the Author

Esther Pia Cordova is on a mission to change mindsets around the world. This change is simple enough: She wants to add the word "yet."

When children say "I can't do that," she adds the word "yet." Esther believes that this simple concept will help children— and adults!—overcome their fears and strive to learn as much as they can in life. One word makes an important difference!

She is the author of the Growth Mindset picture book series, which includes *I Can't Do That, YET*; *A World without Failures*; *Little Bears Can Do Big Things*; and *Your Thoughts Matter*. These books help kids embrace a growth mindset in a fun and engaging way.

For practical ways to help your child's mindset, follow Esther at PowerOfYet.com.